15 REASONS
Why Things Happen

*Navigating the Adversities
and Conflicts of Life*

Darril Deaton

WESTBOW
P R E S S®
A DIVISION OF THOMAS NELSON
& ZONDERVAN

Scripture quotations marked HCSB are taken from the Holman Christian Standard Bible®, Copyright © 1999, 2000, 2002, 2003, 2009 by Holman Bible Publishers. Used by permission. Holman Christian Standard Bible®, Holman CSB®, and HCSB® are federally registered trademarks of Holman Bible Publishers.

Scripture quotations taken from the Holy Bible, New Living Translation, Copyright © 1996, 2004. Used by permission of Tyndale House Publishers, Inc., Wheaton, Illinois 60189. All rights reserved.

Scripture taken from the New King James Version. Copyright © 1979, 1980, 1982 by Thomas Nelson, Inc. Used by permission. All rights reserved.

Scripture quotations are from The Holy Bible, English Standard Version® (ESV®), copyright © 2001 by Crossway, a publishing ministry of Good News Publishers. Used by permission. All rights reserved.

Scripture taken from the Holy Bible, NEW INTERNATIONAL VERSION®. Copyright © 1973, 1978, 1984, 2011 by Biblica, Inc. All rights reserved worldwide. Used by permission. NEW INTERNATIONAL VERSION® and NIV® are registered trademarks of Biblica, Inc. Use of either trademark for the offering of goods or services requires the prior written consent of Biblica US, Inc.

Scripture quotations taken from the New American Standard Bible®, Copyright © 1960, 1962, 1963, 1968, 1971, 1972, 1973, 1975, 1977, 1995 by The Lockman Foundation. Used by permission. (www.Lockman.org)

WestBow Press books may be ordered through booksellers or by contacting:

WestBow Press
A Division of Thomas Nelson & Zondervan
1663 Liberty Drive
Bloomington, IN 47403
www.westbowpress.com
1 (866) 928-1240

ISBN: 978-1-5127-5563-3 (sc)
ISBN: 978-1-5127-5562-6 (e)

Library of Congress Control Number: 2016914636

Print information available on the last page.

WestBow Press rev. date: 09/15/2016

Dedication

This book is dedicated to Jesus Christ and to the family He has given me. To my wife, Dawn, and my children, Denise Smith, and her husband, Curtis, and Darin and his wife, Alexis. To my church family that first heard these principles preached and then encouraged me to write this book.

I also dedicate this book to the people who brought conflict, pain, and adversity into my life. While you may have meant it for harm, God meant it for good. God used even you to shape my understanding and teach me the principles found in this book. For that, and for you, I give God thanks.

I wouldn't be who I am without the people God put in my life.

Contents

Dedication..v
Foreword.. xi
Introduction...xiii

Part 1
Where Do Bad Things Come From?

1. Sin, the Consequences of Your Own
    Carnal Living and Worldly Attitudes, Is
    a Source of Adversity 3
2. Satan Is Also a Constant Source of
    Conflict Because He Hates You 5
3. God Is Also a Source of Your Conflict
    and Adversity Because He Loves You 7

Part 2
Fifteen Reasons Why Things Happen

1. Things Happen to Bring You into
    Conformity with the Image of Jesus Christ............ 11
2. God Will Often Use Conflict and Trials
    to Remind You of His Love for You 15

3. One Reason Things Happen the Way They Do Is to Bring You to a Point of Self-Examination...................................... 19

4. Things May Happen That Would Exhaust Your Resources So You Will Come to Depend on God................................... 21

5. Things May Happen the Way They Do to Make You Humble 25

6. God May Permit Things to Happen the Way They Do So You Will Recognize Your Weaknesses 27

7. God May Allow You to Experience Adversity So You Can Get a Better Knowledge of Him 29

8. Things Happen the Way They Do So You Can Be a Vessel of Comfort and Encouragement to Others 33

9. Things Happen the Way They Do So You Will Come to Hate Evil 37

10. God Uses Adversity to Stretch Your Faith.............. 39

11. God Will Use Your Circumstances to Sift Your Friendships 43

12. Sometimes You May Experience Adversity So That You Will Re-Evaluate Your Priorities 47

13. God May Allow Things to Happen the Way They Do So You Will Not Become Too Attached to Earth... 49

14. We May Experience Adversity and Suffering in Order to Be the Instrument of Deliverance for Others 53

15. God Will Call Believers to Suffer in
    Order to Advance the Gospel.........................57

Part 3
Wrong and Right Ways to Respond to Adversity

Some Wrong Responses to Adversity

1. Don't Find Someone Else To Blame..........................69
2. Don't Fight Against the Adversity..............................71
3. Don't Get Bitter Toward Those Through
   Whom the Adversity Comes 73

The Right Responses to Adversity

1. The First Appropriate Response to
   Adversity Would Be to Examine Yourself...............79
2. When Adversity Comes, Be Sure to
   Commit Yourself to God..83
3. Ask That the Adversity Be Removed........................87
4. In Times of Adversity Go to the Word of God........91
5. You Should Employ the Adversity in
   Ministry to Others...93
6. Whatever You Do, Whatever Happens,
   Praise the Lord!...97

Part 4
Where Do Good Things Come From?

1. God Is the One and Only Source of
   Good Things... 101

2.   Why Does God Give You Anything At All?............ 105

3.   How Should You Respond to the Good
      Things God Gives You?... 107

Final Thoughts.. 111

Foreword

G o into any truck stop or novelty store and you will find a sign that is the equivalent to "Stuff Happens." Why is that sentiment so popular that you can find it immortalized on bumper stickers, buttons, and wooden signs? Well, because stuff happens! Cars break down, ankles get sprained, bad hair days occur, keys get lost, cancer gets diagnosed, dogs throw up on your newly mopped floors, pipes burst, MS symptoms flare up, friends betray, computers crash, and landlords evict their tenants. What happened to the great life of being a Christian?!

Well, God never promised that life would be smooth sailing. In fact, He said quite the opposite. If that's the case, then why in the world would a loving God allow, or even cause, these bad things to happen? It is that very question that is addressed in *Fifteen Reasons Why Things Happen the Way They Do*. The answer may not be as complicated as you might think.

As a Christian and a professional counselor, the concepts in this book have been extremely useful in helping many people understand that God loves you, even in hard times (perhaps especially in hard times), and that He has a plan for it all. God is never caught by surprise, and there are so many hardships we can avoid if we learn what He's teaching the first time around. That way, we avoid repeat lessons.

God has told us many things about adversity, and we need to be well acquainted with His teachings; otherwise we run the risk of responding in a not-so-helpful way. This book is a valuable tool in gaining clarity of God's purpose for adversity as well as what our response should be.

—Denise Smith, LPC, LCDC, VC, MA, BS

Introduction

My father was a preacher of the "old school" variety. After he left to go home, I spent some time going through his old Bibles. I relished the notes he had written in the margins and fly leaves. One such note loosely quoted Paul's words in Romans 8:28-29 with my dad's own personal comment:

> All things work together for good to
> those that love God and respond to
> God's love, call and purpose.
> *It does not say all things are good.*

Our lives on earth are filled with conflicts, adversity, and trouble. This truth is reflected in our music, literature, movies, and books. Christians face the same trials as everyone else. They toil, sweat, bleed, and have headaches, cancer, and debt. Believers are not immune to evil, pain, and spiritual assault. All things are certainly not good.

Scriptures assure us in no uncertain terms that God has a purpose for the life of every single person. If that's true, it means He also has a purpose for the trials and conflicts we endure. But without understanding why things happen the way they do, we waste the whole experience. We go through trials and afflictions that benefit us absolutely nothing. And our testimony to unbelievers reflects poorly on the kingdom of God.

Nothing happens in your life that isn't sifted through God's permissive will first. Yet believers have a stubborn resistance to adversity, often missing God's blessings in the process. This book will help you discover why things happen the way they do and how God would have you respond His way.

I pray that you will experience nothing short of the exciting presence of God as you follow Him through times of adversity as well as times of blessing.

Part 1

Where Do Bad Things Come From?

P eople often ask, "Why is this happening to me?" or "What did I ever do to deserve this?" Joy and sorrow, victory and defeat, fulfillment and disappointment—why do these things happen? There is a divine purpose in the blessings we receive, but there is also this purpose in our heartaches. This is reflected in Paul's letter to the church at Corinth.

> To keep me from becoming conceited because of these surpassingly great revelations, there was given me a thorn in my flesh, a messenger of Satan, to torment me. Three times I pleaded with the Lord to take it away from me. But he said to me, "My grace is sufficient for you, for my power is made perfect in weakness." Therefore I will boast all the more gladly about my weaknesses, so that Christ's power may rest on me. That is why, for Christ's sake, I delight in weaknesses,

> in insults, in hardships, in persecutions, in difficulties. For when I am weak, then I am strong. (2 Corinthians 12:7–10 NIV)

It's helpful to remember that not all Christians are the same. There are basically two kinds of Christians. First, there are believers who are *useful* for God's kingdom. They are becoming disciples, giving sacrificially, praising God continuously, and experiencing an intimate, personal relationship with Christ.

Then there are believers that are *useless* for God's kingdom. They don't serve as they should and don't give as they could. They seldom give praise and rarely have peace or joy. You can be saved and shelved. You can have eternal life and yet, a useless life.

The difference between a useful and useless Christian—a joyful and joyless believer—is not what happens in their lives but how they respond to what happens in their lives! I wonder how many lives will never be influenced by Christ because believers fail to respond correctly to their circumstances. They fail to live crucified lives.

Before you can understand the reasons why things happen the way they do, you must understand some basic principles of God's word. All of your circumstances come from, or are affected by, only three sources.

1

Sin, the Consequences of Your Own Carnal Living and Worldly Attitudes, Is a Source of Adversity

Without sin, you avoid a lot of unnecessary conflict. People are hurting, suffering, and dying all over the world because of somebody's sin. The presence of sin invites adversity. It's the nature of sin to cause adversity. Sin never produces anything good. It never results in your well-being.

Sin is a violation of biblical principles. The Bible outlines principles for living, and things always work best when you refer to the manual and follow the instructions.

> Therefore, since we also have such a large cloud of witnesses surrounding us, let us lay aside every weight and the sin that so easily ensnares us. Let us run with endurance the race that lies before us. (Hebrews 12:1 HCSB)

Sometimes it is the sins of another person that cause your pain and adversity. Someone may punch you in the nose, for example, for no reason at all. It wasn't your sin, but the sin of that other person, that causes you to suffer. Too often we hear stories of abused children, missing persons, and victims of crime or terrorism who suffer due to the sins of others.

When your sin is the source of conflict, however, you can't blame anyone but yourself. You can't blame your childhood, your parents, or your environment. Adam and Eve lived in a perfect world. It was their own sin that was the source of their adversity.

Sin, whether it is yours or someone else's, is a constant source of adversity.

Satan Is Also a Constant Source of Conflict Because He Hates You

You may suffer direct assault by the spiritual forces of evil in the heavenly realms. The devil, however, cannot force you to sin, but he motivates you to sin. This is called *temptation*. Satan always means adversity for your destruction.

As pleasing as his offer may be at times, the devil's ultimate goal is your destruction and embarrassment to God's kingdom. And as alluring as his offer may be, the response is still up to you.

> Be serious! Be alert! Your adversary the Devil is prowling around like a roaring lion, looking for anyone he can devour. (1 Peter 5:8 HCSB)

The devil wants to devour your life, but he doesn't have a lock on it—you can be delivered.

> This poor man cried, and the LORD heard him and saved him from all his troubles. The Angel of

> the LORD encamps around those who fear Him,
> and rescues them. (Psalm 34:6–7 HCSB)

You are engaged in a spiritual conflict, and only spiritual weapons are effective. When you appropriate God's power, even angelic forces get involved. You may not be able to control events, but you can control how you respond to them. An immediate, godly response to Satan's attacks will often shorten or modify the conflict.

3

God Is Also a Source of Your Conflict and Adversity Because He Loves You

The Lord is seeking to accomplish some things in your life, and nothing gets your attention like adversity. He *whispers* in your quiet times—His Spirit to your spirit; He *speaks* in your conscience—your built-in "right-and-wrong meter" but, He *shouts* in your adversity and pain!

> I know, LORD, that Your judgments are just and that You have afflicted me fairly. May Your faithful love comfort me as You promised Your servant. (Psalm 119:75–76 HCSB)

God affects your circumstances in two ways. First, He *causes the circumstances* by direct, deliberate action. Or second, He may also *allow* Satan or sin to affect and influence your circumstances. Whether God causes it or allows it, no conflict happens that isn't a part of His plan for your life.

Adversity must be painful enough to get your attention. It must be beyond your control to stop it, and it must be beyond your ability to manage it. God always means adversity for our good. He is in the thick of your trouble, making it work out for your good and His glory.

Adversity and affliction may sharpen your spiritual senses. People tend to become more alert to spiritual things in the midst of trials. Because of adversity, you may turn to God for the first time in ages and listen for His voice. You may sense an urging to return to prayer, to get back in the Bible, to go to church, and to ask other believers for prayer.

> Although the Lord gives you the bread of adversity and the water of affliction, your teachers will be hidden no more; with your own eyes you will see them. Whether you turn to the right or to the left, your ears will hear a voice behind you, saying, "This is the way; walk in it." (Isaiah 30:20–21 NIV)

God is far more interested in building your character than in solving your problems. We tend to focus on the immediate circumstances, but God sees the big picture. He keeps the main thing, the main thing.

Regardless of the source of your adversities, all your conflicts must be sifted through the permissive will of God first. Nothing happens in the life of a child of God that doesn't cross God's desk first! No matter where your conflicts come from, God is always the outcome!

Part 2

Fifteen Reasons Why Things Happen

We know that there are three sources for the bad things that happen in your life: sin, Satan, and God. Of course, every circumstance is sifted through the permissive will of God first. You can be assured that there is a divine plan for everything that happens in your life.

There is, however, only one source of good things. God, and God alone, is the source of anything good in this sin-wrecked world. He loves you so much that you are the recipient of His grace and salvation. Jesus died for you because of God's great love. We'll discuss this more fully in part 4.

These are the sources of good and bad things, but if God's permissive will allows something to happen, there must be a reason. The Bible reveals that there are at least fifteen reasons why things happen the way they do. Being aware of God's purposes in your conflicts will help you understand His wisdom, love, and purpose for your life.

1

Things Happen to Bring You into Conformity with the Image of Jesus Christ

We know that all things work together for the good of those who love God: those who are called according to His purpose. For those He foreknew He also predestined to be conformed to the image of His Son, so that He would be the firstborn among many brothers. (Romans 8:28–29 HCSB)

Without a doubt, Jesus's life was filled with adversity. Herod tried to take Jesus's life soon after He was born. As a result, His family had to travel the perilous road to Egypt and live in exile for a number of years. When Jesus began His ministry, Satan came to Him in the Judean wilderness, tempting and testing Him, trying to derail the Lord's ministry before it even started. Throughout His life, Jesus faced religious legalism and opposition from powerful men. He was betrayed or abandoned by friends. He endured a series of harsh and illegal trials followed by suffering and vicious torture. Then, as if that weren't enough, Jesus was crucified, suffering in your place and paying for your sins and the sins of the whole world.

What makes Jesus our true Christ is the cross. All the people He fed, all the miracles He performed, all the sick people He healed, and all the great teachings were astounding. But these things were bound to happen in His wake as He passed through. It's the cross that made Him the Savior and demonstrated God's love. It's the cross that set Jesus apart from all other prophets, preachers, seers, and religious leaders.

The cross of Christ is our example to follow. How can we possibly be in the image of Christ without the cross? How can you expect to reflect the grace and love of Christ with a conflict-free life? You can't follow in the steps of Christ without experiencing adversity.

> For you were called to this, because Christ also suffered for you, leaving you an example, so that you should follow in His steps. (1 Peter 2:21 HCSB)

God's greatest power was not manifested in Christ's strength but in His weakest hour. As it turns out, it's that way for you and me. Paul related his own experience with these words:

> Concerning this severe adversity, I pleaded with the Lord three times to take it away from me. But

He said to me, "My grace is sufficient for you, for power is perfected in weaknesses." Therefore, I will most gladly boast all the more about my weaknesses, so that Christ's power may reside in me. (2 Corinthians 12:8–9 HCSB)

It seems that Christians want the power of God in their lives but without trials and conflict. But it's not going to happen! Taking up a cross is God's plan and purpose for His people. A cross means pain, conflict, and adversity.

Then He said to them all, "If anyone wants to come with Me, he must deny himself, take up his cross daily, and follow Me." (Luke 9:23 HCSB)

Jesus could not just skip the agony of the cross and go straight to the empty tomb. He knew there had to be a dark Friday before a victorious Sunday.

The cross defined for all time who Jesus is, Lord and Savior. And the cross defines who you are, His follower. You are to bear the likeness of Jesus in eternity, but it begins here and now.

Earthly people are like the earthly man, and heavenly people are like the heavenly man. Just as we are now like the earthly man, we will someday be like the heavenly man. (1 Corinthians 15:48–49 NLT)

God is trying to conform you to the image of Christ. He desires for you to be like Jesus. He is molding you and making you into the image of His Son. It can't be done without a cross! Why do things happen the way they do? To make you like Jesus.

2

God Will Often Use Conflict and Trials to Remind You of His Love for You

And you have forgotten the exhortation that addresses you as sons: My son, do not take the Lord's discipline lightly or faint when you are reproved by Him, for the Lord disciplines the one He loves and punishes every son He receives. (Hebrews 12:5–6 HCSB)

Discipline usually results in adversity. The "whippings" I received as child seemed pretty adverse at the time because discipline is always unpleasant. But I knew my parents loved me.

Discipline is not the same thing as punishment. The purpose of punishment is to exact retribution for a wrong done. The purpose of discipline is to bring about repentance and change. Punishment is a result of judgment; discipline is a result of mercy.

Discipline is not a means to exact retribution but to assure repentance and a restoration of relationships. Christians, of all people, should seek restoration:

> Brothers, if someone is caught in any wrongdoing, you who are spiritual should restore such a person with a gentle spirit, watching out for yourselves so you also won't be tempted. (Galatians 6:1 HCSB)

Godly discipline is always associated with love, not anger or hate.

> As many as I love, I rebuke and discipline. So be committed and repent. (Revelation 3:19 HCSB)

Rebuke and discipline sound a lot like adversity and conflict to me. But God assures us that love is His motivation. The reason the government makes rules about parental discipline, and tries to limit a parent's role in discipline, is because the government doesn't love your child like a parent should. But God is your heavenly Father, and He loves you deeply like a parent should.

Because of Jesus, God does not deal with you on the basis of your guilt for the things you've done. That's certainly a good thing for you. If you embrace Christ as your Savior and believe that He bled and died for you, and that He returned from the grave to give you life, then you are His child. The fact is, He loves you and deals with you on the basis of His mercy.

> There is no fear in love; instead, perfect love drives out fear, because fear involves punishment. So the one who fears has not reached perfection in love. (1 John 4:18 HCSB)

As a child of God, you need never fear punishment again. All the punishment you deserve was taken out on Jesus Christ. Any conflict you face now could be the result of God's love correcting you.

God is not waiting to "zap" you every time you make a mistake. But He will use discipline to lead you into conformity with the image of Jesus Christ. He loves you and wants what is ultimately the best for you. Adversity, on any level, may be used by God to discipline you and should remind you of God's love, for He disciplines those He loves.

3

One Reason Things Happen the Way They Do Is to Bring You to a Point of Self-Examination

> Search me, God, and know my heart; test me and know my concerns. See if there is any offensive way in me; lead me in the everlasting way. (Psalm 139:23–24 HCSB)

A student may spend many hours studying and preparing for an examination. He may ask, "What have I learned that's important?" or "What do I need to learn that's important?" The purpose of a test given at school is to find out what the student knows, not what the teacher knows.

Don't think that testing comes so God can find out the true condition of your heart. This is not the case, for God already knows the condition of your heart! Testing comes so that God can show you the condition of your heart.

Adversity doesn't show God anything about you. It shows you about God and that He is lovingly conforming you into the image of Christ. In adversity you learn the truth about the depth and strength of your faith. It is in times of conflict that you can find out what you are made of.

Is your faith resting in the power of God? You may never know without conflict and the threat of adversity. It's easy to "walk the walk" when there's no opposition or adversity.

> When all the Israelite men saw Goliath, they retreated from him terrified. … Then David said, "The LORD who rescued me from the paw of the lion and the paw of the bear will rescue me from the hand of this Philistine." Saul said to David, "Go, and may the LORD be with you." (1 Samuel 17:24, 37 HCSB)

David knew from the experiences of past conflict that God could, and would, give him victory over the enemy, Goliath.

You may attend church, quote the Bible, and put on a good Christian front, but are you steeped in faith? You quote the Bible, but do you really trust it? Do you fall apart in the face of adversity?

One reason God may allow certain things to happen in your life is to draw your attention to your heart. You may say that Jesus is Lord, but strife and affliction expose the real truth. Conflict shows you what you are made of. It shows the real substance of your faith. You will never know the depth and strength of your faith until your faith is under fire!

4

Things May Happen That Would Exhaust Your Resources So You Will Come to Depend on God

> The LORD is my shepherd; there is nothing I lack. He lets me lie down in green pastures; He leads me beside quiet waters. He renews my life; He leads me along the right paths for His name's sake. Even when I go through the darkest valley, I fear no danger, for You are with me; Your rod and Your staff—they comfort me. (Psalm 23:1–4 HCSB)

Is there ever a time that you just let Jesus be your Shepherd without being second-guessed by you? Have you really come to a place in your life where you are able to fully trust Him? When you're physically exhausted, experiencing illness, finances are tight, you're without a job, a loved one has died, or your family is facing a crisis of some kind, do you really depend on God?

The staff and rod that the Psalmist talks about is used for both guidance and discipline. The staff, or hooked end, is used for guidance and rescue. The rod, or straight end, is used for discipline.

Have you ever seen the painting in which Jesus is carrying a lamb around His shoulders? It's a picture of discipline. Sheep that stray too far, too often, have their legs broken by the shepherd's rod. That way it becomes necessary for the sheep to depend entirely upon the shepherd until the legs are healed. God wants you to depend upon Him entirely.

An abundance of resources, for example, will often tempt you to be too self-sufficient.

> Because you say, 'I'm rich; I have become wealthy and need nothing,' and you don't know that you are wretched, pitiful, poor, blind, and naked, I advise you to buy from Me gold refined in the fire so that you may be rich, white clothes so that you may be dressed and your shameful nakedness not be exposed, and ointment to spread on your eyes so that you may see. As many as I love, I rebuke and discipline. So be committed and repent. (Revelation 3:17–19 HCSB)

There's nothing wrong with making money or having worldly possessions … unless it separates you from God.

> For the love of money is a root of all kinds of evil, and by craving it, some have wandered away from the faith and pierced themselves with many pains. (1 Timothy 6:10 HCSB)

Did you know that some Christians rob from God?

> Will man rob God? Yet you are robbing me. But you say, 'How have we robbed you?' In your tithes and contributions. You are cursed with a curse, for you are robbing me ... Bring the full tithe into the storehouse, that there may be food in my house. And thereby put me to the test, says the LORD of hosts, if I will not open the windows of heaven for you and pour down for you a blessing until there is no more need. I will rebuke the devourer for you, so that it will not destroy the fruits of your soil, and your vine in the field shall not fail to bear, says the LORD of hosts. (Malachi 3:8–11 ESV)

God's plan for giving financed the ministry of the temple, helped the poor, and assured that the teaching of His truth would continue unabated. Tithes and offerings helped to finance the place of worship and ministry. When the people failed to obey, the ministry suffered, and so did the people who robbed God in the process.

It's amazing how people in our day expect God's blessing when they are stingy in their giving. They expect God to remove whatever curses their financial life, and even expect answered prayer, when all along they are stealing from Him. They live in disobedience to Him but want His blessings.

Sometimes God will exhaust your resources so you will come to depend on Him; obey Him; and be blessed in the process.

But resources go beyond just money and property. What about physical energy, mental sharpness, and emotional balance? Have you ever been worn out from work, stress, and one trial after another? God may bring you to the end of your rope so that you'll learn to hang onto Him.

There are times when things must be taken away, or come up missing, in order for the Lord to fill the void.

> For we do not want you to be unaware, brothers, of the affliction we experienced in Asia. For we were so utterly burdened beyond our strength that we despaired of life itself. Indeed, we felt that we had received the sentence of death. But *that was to make us rely not on ourselves but on God* who raises the dead. He delivered us from such a deadly peril, and he will deliver us. On him we have set our hope that he will deliver us again. (2 Corinthians 1:8–10 ESV)

God may just exhaust all your resources so you will come to depend upon Him. Many times believers fail to experience the vast resources of God because they depend so much on themselves.

5

Things May Happen the Way They Do to Make You Humble

> He mocks those who mock, but gives grace to the humble. (Proverbs 3:34 NASB)

God wants to give you power. He really does. He wants to demonstrate His awesome power in your life. In the Bible the word *grace* is associated with divine power. When you pray for power, and you should, God may first humble you. He may have to bring you to a place to receive His power. And that's where trials, adversity, and trouble come in.

Adversity may be the very thing that will bring you to your knees, and that may be right where God wants you! James put it like this:

> He gives greater grace. Therefore He says: God resists the proud, but gives grace to the humble. ... Be miserable and mourn and weep. Your laughter must change to mourning and your joy to sorrow. Humble yourselves before

the Lord, and He will exalt you. (James 4:6,
9–10 HCSB)

What does it take to experience the power of God
in your life? It may be through the humility, perhaps
even the humiliation that accompanies trouble. It
can be even small things that happen to you that God
can use. For example, sometimes through my own
awkwardness I have tripped on seemingly nothing and
stumbled in public. It may not be a big deal, but it's a little
embarrassing. So at that moment I say a silent prayer
and thank God for His protection and then ask for grace.
That's right, grace. That moment of embarrassment, or
humiliation, put me in a rather humble position. That
could be the very time and place that God would give
me grace. So I want to take advantage of that moment
of humility.

God gives grace to the humble. That's why adverse
circumstances may occur in your life. Adversity, on any
level, great or small, puts you right at the place where
God can give you His grace.

6

God May Permit Things to Happen the Way They Do So You Will Recognize Your Weaknesses

> For the sake of Christ, then, I am content with weaknesses, insults, hardships, persecutions, and calamities. For when I am weak, then I am strong. (2 Corinthians 12:10 ESV)

From all indications Paul suffered from a physical weakness, but God used it to point out a spiritual weakness. Through the trial of physical suffering Paul realized he had not been trusting God to sustain him and hold him up in adversity.

God's strength is magnified in human weakness. When you realize your weaknesses, you put yourself in a position to receive the power of God in astounding ways.

Learn to live out of your weaknesses, not out of your own personal abilities. Unless you are aware of your weaknesses, you may never let God work through them. Adversity is a sharp reminder that you are merely human, and that you have weaknesses, so that the power of God can be manifested in and through your life.

7

God May Allow You to Experience Adversity So You Can Get a Better Knowledge of Him

> This is eternal life: that they may know You, the
> only true God, and the One You have sent—Jesus
> Christ. (John 17:3 HCSB)

The word *know* in this passage indicates an experiential kind of knowledge, not just an intellectual acceptance of a higher power. Salvation is not in having head knowledge that there is a God but a personal relationship with a living, loving, personal Savior. It's a relationship that leads to a deeper understanding of God's character, of God's ways, and of God's love. God wants you to know Him on a deeper, more intimate level. Through adversity you come to know God in ways that would otherwise be missed.

David experienced things in adversity and conflict that led to a new understanding of God's greatness. He saw things about God that He would never see without distress and affliction:

> I waited patiently for the LORD to help me, and he turned to me and heard my cry. He lifted me out of the pit of despair, out of the mud and the mire. He set my feet on solid ground and steadied me as I walked along. He has given me a new song to sing, a hymn of praise to our God. Many will see what he has done and be amazed. They will put their trust in the LORD ... O LORD my God, you have performed many wonders for us. Your plans for us are too numerous to list. You have no equal. If I tried to recite all your wonderful deeds, I would never come to the end of them. (Psalm 40:1–3, 5 NLT)

Without adversity we often have a small, out-of-balance view of God. How could David say, "Though I walk through the valley of the shadow of death You are with me," unless he had actually walked through the valley of the shadow of death? He would not have known God's loving presence without the trial of going through the valley. You can read the truth, proclaim the truth, and even believe the truth, but it really isn't yours until you have experienced God in adversity.

Stephen gave His life for Christ. He experienced the adversity of an unjust trial and persecution, yet in the midst of it he saw Christ in a way he had never experienced before:

The Jewish leaders were infuriated by Stephen's accusation, and they shook their fists at him in rage. But Stephen, full of the Holy Spirit, gazed steadily into heaven and saw the glory of God, and he saw Jesus standing in the place of honor at God's right hand. And he told them, "Look, I see the heavens opened and the Son of Man standing in the place of honor at God's right hand!" (Acts 7:54–56 NLT)

You read about people in the Bible that the Lord rescued or helped in some way. And there are Christians around the world who testify to God's grace and deliverance through persecution and hardship. It's natural to ask, "Would God do the same for me if I were in the same place?" Or, "Would God calm a stormy sea for me if I were sinking?" You will never know unless you find yourself in a storm-tossed boat!

Without conflict and adversity, you could not see the advocacy side of God. Without trials and afflictions, you would not know just how secure you really are inside His hedge of protection. There's just no other way to know God on the deepest, most intimate level like when you experience trouble, pain, and conflict in your life. It may be that God just wants you to know Him better.

8

Things Happen the Way They Do So You Can Be a Vessel of Comfort and Encouragement to Others

> All praise to God, the Father of our Lord Jesus Christ. God is our merciful Father and the source of all comfort. He comforts us in all our troubles so that we can comfort others. When they are troubled, we will be able to give them the same comfort God has given us. (2 Corinthians 1:3–4 NLT)

You learn some valuable "pass-along" lessons about God, life, and love in adversity. If you are a follower of Christ, you are doing others a disservice if you are not ministering the comfort and truth you learned in times of adversity. It is just plain wrong to be comforted, or to learn a new spiritual truth, and not use it for the benefit of others.

Difficulties and hardships actually *train you*, and *qualify you*, to care for others. God doesn't just minister to you to resolve your conflicts but so you have the qualifications and experience to minister to others in their conflicts. Use the comfort and assurances you received in your darkest days to minister to others.

You are also a vessel of encouragement to others when you let them bless you. There are times when you need to let others care for you, use their gifts, share their resources, and lift you up in prayer. God may use your conflicts to prompt the loving service of others.

> I rejoiced in the Lord greatly that once again you renewed your care for me. You were, in fact, concerned about me but lacked the opportunity to show it. I don't say this out of need, for I have learned to be content in whatever circumstances I am. I know both how to have a little, and I know how to have a lot. In any and all circumstances I have learned the secret of being content — whether well fed or hungry, whether in abundance or in need. I am able to do all things through Him who strengthens me. Still, you did well by sharing with me in my hardship. (Philippians 4:10–14 HCSB)

Perhaps you have denied others the blessing of ministry by discouraging their care for your needs. Reasons you might give are "I didn't want to bother you," or "I don't want anyone to go to any trouble." You may not want people to be bothered, but they need to be bothered. How can people love their neighbor if their neighbor is not open to their help? Sometimes we want to be so self-sufficient that we are too proud to admit we need help.

If you've experienced God's presence in adversity then you aren't just *qualified* to comfort others, you are *required* to comfort others and minister in Jesus's name. But at the same time, you must let others minister to you and share God's love with you. Either way, you are called to be a vessel of comfort to others out of your own experiences and adversity.

9

Things Happen the Way They Do So You Will Come to Hate Evil

> Abhor what is evil; hold fast to what is good.
> (Romans 12:9b ESV)

It is hard to comprehend how offensive evil is in the presence of a holy God. It is so offensive, in fact, that when Jesus took all your sins on the cross, God would no longer look on Him. God abhors evil and would have us hate it, too.

Satan says the program is contentment and getting by with as few difficulties as possible. The result is a demand for instant pleasure and worldly gratification. The Internet puts lust gratification at a person's fingertips. The craving for drugs, sex, and R-rated entertainment reflect man's addiction to evil desires. The desire to gossip and pass along juicy tidbits about other people is just as evil. Jesus taught that just the thought of something inappropriate, evil, or coarse is sinful.

The thing is Satan doesn't tell you the consequences of his program! He knows sin will rob you of your joy, of your peace, of your self-esteem, and of your relationship to God.

There is a process that God often uses to get your attention so you'll come *to* hate evil. First, you may receive a verbal reminder—through a message, a Scripture passage, a song, or a friend—that sin is not acceptable in the life of a believer. It serves as a warning of sin's presence and the need to repent.

Second, through the sharpness of adversity, God will get your attention and rivet your mind on the sin you need to turn from. Satan wages his battle in your mind, so it often takes a sharp reminder to get your attention.

God wants you to purge evil, not protect it!

> O you who love the LORD, hate evil! (Psalm 97:10a ESV)

It takes the fire of adversity to focus your attention on the gravity of sin and evil. It has to be intense enough for you to come to hate evil.

> Let love be genuine. Abhor what is evil; hold fast to what is good. (Romans 12:9 ESV)

You ought to hate sin because of how much people suffer from it. You should also hate it because it offends God. But at least you should hate it because it causes you pain and adversity.

10

God Uses Adversity to Stretch Your Faith

By faith Abraham obeyed when he was called to go out to a place that he was to receive as an inheritance. And he went out, not knowing where he was going. By faith he went to live in the land of promise, as in a foreign land, living in tents with Isaac and Jacob, heirs with him of the same promise. By faith Abraham, when he was tested, offered up Isaac, and he who had received the promises was in the act of offering up his only son, of whom it was said, "Through Isaac shall your offspring be named." He considered that God was able even to raise him from the dead, from which, figuratively speaking, he did receive him back. And what more shall I say? For time would fail me to tell of Gideon ... of David and Samuel and the prophets — who through faith conquered kingdoms, enforced justice, obtained promises, stopped the mouths of lions, quenched the power of fire, escaped the edge of the sword, were made strong out of weakness, became mighty in war, put foreign armies to flight. Women received back their dead by resurrection. Some were tortured, refusing to accept release, so that they might rise again to a better life. Others suffered mocking and flogging, and even chains and imprisonment. They were stoned, they were sawn in two, they were killed with the sword. They went about in skins of sheep and goats, destitute, afflicted, mistreated — of whom the world was not worthy — wandering about in deserts and mountains, and in dens and caves of the earth. And all these, though commended through their faith, did not receive what was promised ... (Hebrews 11:8–9; 17–19; 32–39 ESV)

God will lead you through experiences that test and stretch your faith. As a loving Father, God wants you to grow, so He exercises your faith. Many believers expect their "saving faith" to carry them through the adversities of life. But the faith you held as a babe in Christ will not get you through the tribulations and warfare of life.

Abraham's faith was stretched to its limits. He left the security of home, family, and familiar surroundings and journeyed into the unknown. His faith had more depth after this and other experiences. Eventually, he was called upon to offer up his son, Isaac. He had the faith to tell his son that God would provide a sacrifice. The sum total of all his experiences with God through adversity must have brought Abraham to a new level of faith. I imagine as he climbed that hill with Isaac that he was repeating to himself, "God will provide; God will provide; God will provide." After all, God always came through.

God has tested the faith of many others. Time and again their faith was stretched to the limit with severe trails and distress. Many great saints of God had their faith stretched through adversity. It's not just one or two heroes of the faith but many people, past and present, whose faith has been stretched to new levels of confidence. God stretches your faith, too, again and again, each time leading you to a new plateau of faith. This is exactly how spiritual growth occurs.

When believers take the easy road, or the path of least resistance, or avoid stepping out of their comfort zone, spiritual growth is stunted. Remember that David's experience serves as a perfect model for us. He explained to the king why he was confident he would defeat Goliath:

> And David said, "The LORD who delivered me from the paw of the lion and from the paw of the bear will deliver me from the hand of this Philistine." And Saul said to David, "Go, and the LORD be with you!" (1 Samuel 17:37 ESV)

David would never have faced Goliath without the confidence that had grown out of past experience.

When you come to a place in your life where you are willing to follow Christ and trust Him for the next step, God can begin to stretch and refine your faith. He wants to become your point of reference — to teach you to live a supernatural life in a natural world. So God will pull you, and stretch you, so your faith and confidence with grow.

11

God Will Use Your Circumstances to Sift Your Friendships

The friends and associations you choose are very important. Friends can be an influence for good or evil. They can be a help or a hindrance to your spiritual growth. They may join you in life's battles or make the way tougher.

One of the great friendships of all time was that of David and Jonathan. Below are selected passages from 1 Samuel 19 and 20 that describe their friendship.

> And Saul spoke to Jonathan his son and to all his servants, that they should kill David. But Jonathan, Saul's son, delighted much in David. And Jonathan told David, "Saul my father seeks to kill you. Therefore be on your guard in the morning. Stay in a secret place and hide yourself. (1 Samuel 19:1–2 ESV)

> Then David ... said before Jonathan, "What have I done? What is my guilt? And what is my sin

before your father, that he seeks my life?" And he said to him, "Far from it! You shall not die. Behold, my father does nothing either great or small without disclosing it to me. And why should my father hide this from me? It is not so." But David vowed again, saying, "Your father knows well that I have found favor in your eyes, and he thinks, 'Do not let Jonathan know this, lest he be grieved.' But truly, as the LORD lives and as your soul lives, there is but a step between me and death." Then Jonathan said to David, "Whatever you say, I will do for you." (1 Samuel 20:1–4 ESV)

Then Saul's anger was kindled against Jonathan ... send and bring him to me, for he shall surely die." Then Jonathan answered Saul his father, "Why should he be put to death? What has he done?" (1 Samuel 20:30–32 ESV)

[Later] Then Jonathan said to David, "Go in peace, because we have sworn both of us in the name of the LORD, saying, 'The LORD shall be between me and you, and between my offspring and your offspring, forever.'" And he rose and departed, and Jonathan went into the city. (1 Samuel 20:42 ESV)

David was running for his life. He found himself separated from family, friends, and possessions. The entire military was looking to kill him. Now that's conflict!

Conflict will put a strain on any friendship. And there came a time when Jonathan had to choose between David or his own father. That only added to the conflict that could have torn their friendship apart.

The result of Jonathan's decision to remain loyal to his friend preserved the future king of Israel and protected the Messianic line. This was one of the greatest friendships of all time.

Adversity will sift out those friends that are not true blue. You know, the "fair weather" variety of friends. Friendships that have been sifted and shaped through adversity will not be weakened by distance, time, or circumstances.

12

Sometimes You May Experience Adversity So That You Will Re-Evaluate Your Priorities

> Therefore, do not be anxious, saying, 'What shall we eat?' or 'What shall we drink?' or 'What shall we wear?' For the Gentiles seek after all these things, and your heavenly Father knows that you need them all. But seek first the kingdom of God and his righteousness, and all these things will be added to you. (Matthew 6:31–33 ESV)

Make a list: Family, marriage, job, church, recreation, Bible study, personal appearance, romance, rest and relaxation, video games, TV, and movies. Which ones are your priorities?

Jesus said to put the kingdom of God first, ahead of everything and everyone else. A kingdom has to do with rule and authority. It relates to the priority of one who is a citizen of that kingdom. The word Jesus used for righteousness has to do with one's attitude toward

God. Are God and His character really important to you? What priority does Christ's rule and righteousness have in your life?

Many times people on their deathbed (definitely a time of conflict and anxiety) confess a life of confused or self-centered priorities. But then it's too late to avoid unnecessary conflict and loss.

Adversity will certainly cause you to reevaluate your priorities and help you determine what is really important.

> Brothers, I do not consider that I have made it my own. But one thing I do: forgetting what lies behind and straining forward to what lies ahead, I press on toward the goal for the prize of the upward call of God in Christ Jesus. Let those of us who are mature think this way … (Philippians 3:13–15 ESV)

Conflict will test your priorities. So you can see why God would use adversity in your life. He may want you to reexamine what's truly important.

13

God May Allow Things to Happen the Way They Do So You Will Not Become Too Attached to Earth

These all died in faith without having received the promises, but they saw them from a distance, greeted them, and confessed that they were foreigners and temporary residents on the earth. ... But they now desire a better place — a heavenly one. Therefore, God is not ashamed to be called their God, for He has prepared a city for them. (from Hebrews 11:13–16 HCSB)

As a believer you should understand that there's more to living than just the few years you have on earth. Christ-followers are not completely happy here because they're not supposed to be! Many Christians have foolishly concluded that because they were born on earth, live on earth, and interact with the world that it's their home. But it's not. Your time on earth is a temporary assignment.

> Dear friends, I warn you as "temporary residents and foreigners" to keep away from worldly desires that wage war against your very souls. (1 Peter 2:11 NLT)

When you remember this, your values will be radically altered. Eternal values will become the deciding factors for all your decisions. When you remember that life on earth is really a test, a trust, and just a temporary assignment, the appeal of worldly things will lose their hold on your life.

You will never feel completely satisfied on earth because you were made for more. God will allow you, as a Christian, to experience adversity and conflict so that you will be discontented and dissatisfied with the world. He wants you to focus your values and attachments on eternal things and look toward your real home.

> Therefore, we do not give up. Even though our outer person is being destroyed, our inner person is being renewed day by day. For our momentary light affliction is producing for us an absolutely incomparable eternal weight of glory. So we do not focus on what is seen, but on what is unseen. For what is seen is temporary, but what is unseen is eternal. (2 Corinthians 4:16–18 HCSB)

You may spend years struggling with conflict, adversity, turmoil, and discontentment. That's the nature of life on earth. All the while your loving heavenly Father has been drawing your attention and your affection toward the only things that matter.

When life is hard and you just feel overwhelmed, or when you wonder if living for Jesus is really worth it, just remind yourself, "I'm not home yet!"

14

We May Experience Adversity and Suffering in Order to Be the Instrument of Deliverance for Others

God may use you to save others. This will always be a source of conflict, suffering, and pain. To what lengths are you willing to go in order to save a loved one, a friend, or maybe even a stranger?

Joseph had suffered unfair and humiliating treatment. He was betrayed by His own brothers; separated from a father that loved him; falsely accused of sexual impropriety; and imprisoned for years with little hope of freedom. Anytime along the way he could have given up on God and given in to the temptations of the world. How easy and "normal" it would be to give in to the advances of another man's wife and do what comes "naturally" in that situation.

On top of that, it seemed that Joseph's faith and allegiance to God were the very source of his conflicts. He didn't suffer for doing wrong; he suffered for doing right! He didn't deserve all the trials, trouble, and misery. Yet, God used adversity to stretch Joseph's faith over the years and get him in the perfect position to accomplish a divine purpose. Look what Joseph told his brothers:

> God sent me ahead of you to establish you as a remnant within the land and to keep you alive by a great deliverance. Therefore, it was not you who sent me here, but God. (Genesis 45:7–8 HCSB)

Joseph came to realize two things. First, he realized that God had a specific purpose in saving generations of men and women from certain death and disaster, and second, that it could have all been for nothing if he had given in, given up, and simply blamed others for his problems.

Mary, Jesus's mother, also suffered a lot so others could be saved. I doubt she understood the full ramification of her faith at the beginning.

> Joseph also went up from the town of Nazareth in Galilee, to Judea … to be registered along with Mary, who was engaged to him and was pregnant. While they were there, the time came for her to give birth. Then she gave birth to her firstborn Son, and she wrapped Him snugly in cloth and laid Him in a feeding trough—because there was no room for them at the lodging place. (Luke 2:4–7 HCSB)

We always remember the beautiful angels, the majestic magi, and the soft, glorious events surrounding

Jesus's birth. But what about the shame of an unwed pregnancy? What about the long, arduous trip while being with child, having no reservations and sleeping in a barn, not to mention giving birth there? And there were no parents nearby to help or rejoice with her. That's not to mention the escape to a foreign country to save her child. Life was not easy for Mary.

But that's not even the worst part of her trials.

> Standing by the cross of Jesus were His mother, His mother's sister, Mary the wife of Clopas, and Mary Magdalene. When Jesus saw His mother and the disciple He loved standing there, He said to His mother, "Woman, here is your son." Then He said to the disciple, "Here is your mother." And from that hour the disciple took her into his home. (John 19:25–27 HCSB)

Mary endured the heartache and distress of watching her son be sentenced to death and then be executed shamefully on a cross. Yet you have been saved, delivered from your worst sins, because of her afflictions and sacrifice. If you're a believer in Christ, you'll get a chance to thank her.

I haven't even mentioned the conflicts, misery, and distress Jesus suffered for your salvation and deliverance. He remained faithful to the Father in the midst of it all; in spite of it all; and because of it all.

Sometimes you may suffer the loss of reputation, comfort, health, resources, and even life itself. Suffering could continue for a brief time, or for a very long period of time. All the while, you remain unaware that the salvation of others is being purchased by your faithfulness. Yes, you may be the instrument of salvation for someone else ... and that will bring adversity, conflict, and trials.

15

God Will Call Believers to Suffer in Order to Advance the Gospel

> So don't be ashamed of the testimony about our Lord, or of me His prisoner. Instead, share in suffering for the gospel, relying on the power of God. (2 Timothy 1:7–8 HCSB)

> We endure everything so that we will not hinder the gospel of Christ. (1 Corinthians 9:12 HCSB)

The gospel has never been the easy way to live, not for true disciples of Jesus Christ. Suffering has accompanied the proclamation of the gospel in every generation, on every continent, wherever it is preached. The enemies of the gospel would belittle us, embarrass us, and discount our faith. But God would not have us be ashamed of the gospel story or be embarrassed to claim Jesus as Lord.

Incarceration and imprisonment were nothing to be proud of in Paul's day. It meant that some court, some judge, had determined you to be unfit to be live free.

Imprisonment was harsh and bitter and involved great suffering. Yet, Paul wrote a letter from midst of the darkness and pain of imprisonment and declared:

> "I am not ashamed of the power of the gospel ..."and he explains that "it is the power of God unto salvation!" (Romans 1:16 HCSB)

When the gospel is preached, taught, and lived out in the world, God's power is released. Especially for those who are doing the preaching, the teaching, and the living out of the gospel. Paul even calls believers to intentionally share in the suffering that the gospel brings. It's not just something that happens; it's something a true disciple embraces.

Jesus went so far as to give His own life intentionally on the cross. Suffering the ridicule and vitriol of the culture, He endured the incredible pain of crucifixion. But since the gospel is the power of God, Jesus's suffering was followed by the resurrection from the grave. And it has resulted in the salvation of millions of people who believe in Him and have embraced the gospel of God's power.

Jesus tried to prepare His followers from the outset what the cost might be to advance the gospel:

> For whoever wants to save his life will lose it, but whoever loses his life because of Me and the gospel will save it. (Mark 8:35 HCSB)

The gospel runs against the grain of our culture; it is contrary to the world. It is, in fact, the light in darkness, and "men love darkness rather than light." So if believers live out the gospel, which is the power of God, it will necessarily cause conflict at the point of contact with the powers of darkness.

> "I assure you," Jesus said, "there is no one who has left house, brothers or sisters, mother or father, children, or fields because of Me and the gospel, who will not receive 100 times more …" (Mark 10:29 HCSB)

> Now I want you to know, brothers, that what has happened to me has actually resulted in the advance of the gospel, so that it has become known throughout the whole imperial guard, and to everyone else, that my imprisonment is in the cause of Christ. (Philippians 1:12–13 HCSB)

All of our suffering can and should advance the gospel. If we demonstrated trust and courage during adversity, whatever the source, a world lost in hopelessness would witness the reality of our loving God. Our lives would give testimony to the gospel that has set us so free.

People should see that believers have a mind that is set on another dimension and fully in love with Jesus Christ. It isn't because He has saved us from experiencing conflict and pain but because He is present with us in the midst of it.

God does not demand that believers suffer for the gospel, but He looks for those who will spread the gospel no matter the suffering, conflict, and adversity it may bring. The question that I ask myself is this: In all the conflicts, adversities, suffering, loss, and tears I have experienced in my life, did any of it advance the gospel of Jesus Christ?

Final Thoughts on the Reasons Why Things Happen

> If anyone speaks, it should be as one who speaks God's words; if anyone serves, it should be from the strength God provides, so that God may be glorified through Jesus Christ in everything. To Him belong the glory and the power forever and ever. Amen. (1 Peter 4:11 HCSB)

No matter what you do—in all circumstances—you must do everything in the strength God provides. No matter what happens to you, no matter why it happens to you, you must depend upon the Lord. He will never leave you, never forsake you.

He allows or causes adversity and conflict in your life in order to penetrate your heart and draw your attention to Himself. God's purpose is to build your character, not to resolve your conflicts. No matter how much adversity you face or how much conflict you experience, trust your Creator to do what is best.

> So those who suffer according to God's will should, while doing what is good, entrust

themselves to a faithful Creator. (1 Peter 4:19 HCSB)

The result should be praise to Jesus Christ, the One in whose image you are being molded day by day, adversity by adversity, one circumstance at a time.

Part 3

Wrong and Right Ways to Respond to Adversity

K nowing the reasons why things happen the way they do is important, but is it more important to know how to respond to adversity. God encourages you to stay the course, remember who you are, and keep your eyes trained on the reward.

Have you forgotten the encouraging words God spoke to you as his children? He said, "My child, don't make light of the LORD's discipline, and don't give up when he corrects you. For the LORD disciplines those he loves, and he punishes each one he accepts as his child." As you endure this divine discipline, remember that God is treating you as his own children. Who ever heard of a child who is never disciplined by its father? If God doesn't discipline you as he does all of his children, means that you are illegitimate and are not really his children at all ... God's discipline is always good for us, so that we might share in his holiness. No discipline is enjoyable while it is happening — it's painful! But afterward there will be a peaceful harvest of right living for those who are trained in this way. So take a new grip with your tired hands and strengthen your weak knees. ... Work at living in peace with everyone, and work at living a holy life, for those who are not holy will not see the Lord. (Hebrews 12:5–14 NLT)

Many believers don't immediately respond to adversity in the right way. They endure tribulation, conflict, and pain without responding to it God's way. They don't consider that God is part of the experience.

You might say that no one has any idea what you're going through. Yet the fact is, the nature or intensity of the adversity is not the issue. The circumstances are not really important. What's important is how you respond. Christ will not reward you according to the nature or intensity of your worldly tribulations. He will reward you according to the nature and quality of your response!

For no one can lay any other foundation than what has been laid down. That foundation is Jesus Christ. If anyone builds on that foundation with gold, silver, costly stones, wood, hay, or straw, each one's work will become obvious, for the day will disclose it, because it will be revealed by fire; the fire will test the quality of each one's work. (1 Corinthians 3:11–13 HCSB)

You will never experience the adversity and conflict that Jesus faced. It was His response to the circumstances that will shine throughout eternity! You, too, are rewarded on the basis of the quality of your works (responses), not the nature or intensity of your conflicts. When you respond the wrong way, in your own abilities and resources, you waste the whole experience. All the pain, suffering, and tears are for nothing!

Some Wrong Responses
to Adversity

I t's in your sinful nature to do things your own way, to react impulsively, and to respond from the flesh. As a result, many of your conflicts are only intensified by the way you respond.

Don't Find Someone Else To Blame

It is a part of your human nature to pass responsibility to others. We live in a society where violence and crime are no longer the perpetrator's fault. It's the environment, or it's their parents, or it's peer pressure, or it's bullying, or momentary weakness, or it was the alcohol, or the drugs. It used to be called shirking your responsibility, passing the buck, or just plain lying. Each one of us, however, is ultimately responsible to the Creator and Judge of the universe. He is the Lawgiver and the One to whom all people will give an account.

> So then, each of us will give an account of himself to God. (Romans 14:12 HCSB)

How you apologize, for example, often reveals your true feelings, or the absence of sincere remorse, and serves as an example of sharing the blame with others. Wrong ways to apologize would be to say, "I'm sorry you were offended," or "I guess we were both wrong," or "I'm sorry you misunderstood me," or the all-time favorite, "If I did anything wrong, please forgive me."

This kind of apology shifts the blame to the other person, or at least makes him or her share in the responsibility. The more of the blame we can shift onto another, the more we shift it off ourselves.

The right way to apologize is take the responsibility for your offense, "I was wrong when I [*name the offense*]. Will you forgive me?"

It will humble you to accept the responsibility and the role you played in the conflict. But that's good. Take the responsibility for the part you may have played and let God forgive you and give you His grace to move on.

God has sifted your conflicts and filtered them through His will. Don't blame and curse God for adversity. Respond the right way and see what God has in mind.

2

Don't Fight Against the Adversity

Instead of resisting God and fighting against His purpose for you, find out what He has in mind. There's a specific reason why God allows you to experience problems and conflicts.

Job is a case study in adversity and appropriate responses. He recognized that everything, good and bad, came through God's will for His life. He also knew that rejecting adversity would be equivalent to rejecting God.

> Job's wife said to him, "Do you still retain your integrity? Curse God and die!" "You speak as a foolish woman speaks," he told her. "Should we accept only good from God and not adversity?" Throughout all this Job did not sin in what he said. (Job 2:9–10 HCSB)

Job, like many of the prophets, did not fight against the adversity, or against God, but committed Himself to God.

> Brothers, take the prophets who spoke in the Lord's name as an example of suffering and patience. See, we count as blessed those who have endured. You have heard of Job's endurance and have seen the outcome from the Lord. The Lord is very compassionate and merciful. (James 5:10–11 HCSB)

God uses adversity and conflict to build your character, to give you a life message and a testimony. You may not become all that God intended for you to be if you resist His working in your life.

I'll use the example of one adversity we've all experienced, the common cold. You cannot cure a cold no matter how you fight against it. The best thing to do is to try and relieve its symptoms the best you can and then just go with the flow. It will come to an end eventually. The benefit of having the distress of a cold is immunization against the same virus—at least for a while. Cold or no cold, you still have to be responsible and go to work and take care of your family. You work through it and do the best you can until it's over.

God uses good things in our lives, but He also uses adversity. Are you willing to take only the good things? Don't you want all God has for you? Then do the best you can. Depend on God. Work through it.

3

Don't Get Bitter Toward Those Through Whom the Adversity Comes

The human tendency is to focus on the instrument of conflict and not the real source. For example, handgun laws are directed at the instrument of adversity but not the real source of the violence. There was hatred, anger, murder, and bullying, along with crimes of passion, long before there were guns. Laws against guns will not change the human heart.

It may help to think of persons who cause you conflict, tears, and heartache as a channel through whom God is working to build your character and draw you closer to Him. Their hearts may be cruel and actions hurtful, but they are unwitting messengers on God's behalf.

The apostle Paul understood that even Satan's worse attacks were actually used by God to help the apostle grow in character. He didn't blame God or the messenger but gladly received God's intended purpose.

> ... so that I would not exalt myself, a thorn in the flesh was given to me, a messenger of Satan to torment me so I would not exalt myself. ... So I take pleasure in weaknesses, insults, catastrophes, persecutions, and in pressures, because of Christ. For when I am weak, then I am strong. (2 Corinthians 12:7, 10 HCSB)

In the old days, when a king didn't like the message he received through a courier, he would kill the courier. Needless to say it didn't change the facts or alter the circumstances. Killing the messenger never changes the message!

Bitterness is never a private sin. It causes turmoil and disruption in the individual, but it also brings division and conflict among the bitter person's sphere of influence. God warns that bitterness will eat people up.

> Look after each other so that none of you fails to receive the grace of God. Watch out that no poisonous root of bitterness grows up to trouble you, corrupting many. (Hebrews 12:15 NLT)

Bitterness will corrupt your heart and your mind. You will fail to experience God's daily grace in your life when you are consumed by bitterness.

Bitterness redirects your focus away from Jesus and toward those who have offended you, hurt you, and caused you pain. And bitterness toward others will surely distract you from following Jesus. You can't keep your eyes on Christ and remain focused on your adversaries.

> Let us run with endurance the race that lies before us ... keeping our eyes on Jesus, the source and perfector of our faith ... (Hebrews 12:1–2 HCSB)

Has someone truly offended you and deliberately hurt you? What if they have gone so far as to make themselves your enemy? What did Jesus say about that?

> I tell you, love your enemies and pray for those who persecute you, so that you may be sons of your Father in heaven. (Matthew 5:44 HCSB)

The heavenly Father sent His Son to die for the sins of His enemies and your enemies, too. Love your enemies (love is an action not a feeling). Pray for them. Don't let bitterness rule in your heart. It will ruin you.

How a Wrong Response May Lead to Unwanted, Unnecessary Conflict

A Wrong Response to Adversity May Result in a Poor Testimony

When you respond the wrong way to adversity, pressure, and stress, you are demonstrating that your God forsakes you. You give others the impression that

God either doesn't care or couldn't help you if He wanted to. He is incapable of meeting your needs. Of course, nothing could be further from the truth, but that's the impression you give others when you respond the wrong way to adversity.

A Wrong Response to Adversity May Invite the Scorn of Others

You invite the hostility of a cynical world when you become angry and bitter toward the God you profess to believe in. And when adversity strikes, if you are as fearful and alarmed as everyone else, you may find yourself to be the object of ridicule.

A Wrong Response May Mean You Get Another Go-Round with Adversity

If you have not responded to God's Word, or failed to repent of your sin, or you have resisted God's grace, you might invite another go-round with conflict. Many believers go through one unnecessary round of adversity after another simply because they don't rightly respond when trouble and conflict come.

The Right Responses
to Adversity

Every believer should desire to be like Jesus, to be conformed to His image, and to become more like Him. And you certainly don't want your adversity and pain to be a wasted experience. Your response to adversity, then, should be deliberate and intentional and follow God's will.

1

The First Appropriate Response to Adversity Would Be to Examine Yourself

> Do not both adversity and good come from the mouth of the Most High? Why should any living person complain, any man, because of the punishment for his sins? Let us search out and examine our ways, and turn back to the LORD. (Lamentations 3:38–40 HCSB)

In times of adversity and conflict, you either become sensitive to spiritual things or hardened to spiritual things. Sometimes the disciples had difficulty getting their minds around the events they experienced. One time, Jesus had miraculously fed a multitude of people from a boy's humble lunch. Later He walked on a stormy sea to the disciples' boat.

They had almost died in that storm. Even with the Lord's presence, they were terrified. They hadn't caught the significance of the day's events and Christ's care for the hungry crowd.

> They were all terrified when they saw him. But Jesus spoke to them at once. "Don't be afraid," he said. "Take courage! I am here!" Then he climbed into the boat, and the wind stopped. They were totally amazed, for *they still didn't understand the significance* of the miracle of the loaves. Their hearts were too hard to take it in. (Mark 6:50–52 NLT)

The disciples had focused on the adversity and forgotten all about the power of Christ. They didn't even recognize Jesus when He came strolling up to the boat. It would have been good for the disciples to examine themselves and ask why they doubted. You need to examine yourself and see if there is an attitude or action that contributed to the intensity and severity of the trial.

Even if there is no sin directly related to the cause, there may be sin that intensifies the conflict. A lot of Christians intensify their trouble, not because of how they act but how they react!

Adversity helps you determine if you have weaknesses and sin tendencies that let Satan get a stronghold in your life. If there are sins or weaknesses that open the door for conflicts and trouble, then you should confess that to God and repent of them.

> … let us lay aside every weight and the sin that so easily ensnares us. Let us run with endurance the

race that lies before us, keeping our eyes on Jesus, the source and perfecter of our faith, who for the joy that lay before Him endured a cross and despised the shame and has sat down at the right hand of God's throne. (Hebrews 12:1–2 HCSB)

Whether adversity is caused by your sin or not, it can turn us away from God. It isn't wrong for you to ask why trouble or trials come; just don't eliminate yourself from the list of possible causes.

Watch out, brothers, so that there won't be in any of you an evil, unbelieving heart that departs from the living God. But encourage each other daily, while it is still called today, so that none of you is hardened by sin's deception. (Hebrews 3:12–13 HCSB)

Don't let adversity harden your heart to God and His ways.

2

When Adversity Comes, Be Sure to Commit Yourself to God

Y ou must respond to all adversity as if it is from God. After all, He sifted it through His will before it got to you. There is no suffering in a believer's life that is apart from God's will.

> So those who suffer according to God's will should, while doing what is good, entrust themselves to a faithful Creator. (1 Peter 4:19 HCSB)

If you focus on Satan, or the agent of adversity, it won't resolve the conflict. Some believers are preoccupied with Satan, evil spirits, and demonic activity. Your focus, however, must be on Jesus. To focus on Christ will help you to affirm your position in Christ. So, remember who you are and that you've been adopted and paid for with the blood of Christ.

> He predestined us to be adopted through Jesus Christ for Himself, according to His favor and

will ... We have redemption in Him through His blood, the forgiveness of our trespasses, according to the riches of His grace. ... We have also received an inheritance in Him, predestined according to the purpose of the One who works out everything in agreement with the decision of His will ... But God, who is rich in mercy, because of His great love that He had for us, made us alive with the Messiah even though we were dead in trespasses. You are saved by grace! Together with Christ Jesus He also raised us up and seated us in the heavens ... But now in Christ Jesus, you who were far away have been brought near by the blood of the Messiah. (Ephesians 1:5–11; 2:4–6, 13 HCSB)

Never, ever forget who you are. Give the Lord every single part of your life. Don't hold back favorite sins, bitterness, personal tastes, innermost desires, and best-laid plans.

Even if the adversity is not removed, you can count on God to keep it from overwhelming you. Just stay committed to Christ no matter what.

Commit your way to the LORD; trust in Him, and He will act ... A man's steps are established by the LORD, and He takes pleasure in his way. Though he falls, he will not be overwhelmed, because the LORD holds his hand. (Psalm 37:5; 23–24 HCSB)

The shepherd, David, had learned as a young boy that commitment to God is honored with His presence and power. It's something that King David never forgot.

3

Ask That the Adversity Be Removed

P aul prayed repeatedly for adversity to be removed.

> So that I would not exalt myself, a thorn in the
> flesh was given to me, a messenger of Satan
> to torment me so I would not exalt myself.
> Concerning this, I pleaded with the Lord three
> times to take it away from me. (2 Corinthians
> 12:7–8 HCSB)

We don't know what Paul's thorn may have been, but
it was severe enough for him to pray repeatedly that it
be removed. God invites you to pray, too, and seek relief
from trials, pain, and difficulty.

Removal, however, may depend on how alert you are
to learning what God is teaching you, or how faithful you
are in correcting your weaknesses. And if the adversity
is removed, it may not be immediate. You may ask why
doesn't God just solve the conflict and receive all the
glory for it. Don't make the assumption that God is
glorified in your deliverance. Sometimes He is glorified

more in your adversity and pain. Remember, Paul invited weakness, sickness, and conflict once he realized it invited overwhelming grace.

Jesus personally glorified God in His suffering and death, but He was not delivered from the cross. God's greatest and loftiest purpose required the cross, the suffering, and the death of His own Son. Even Jesus's prayer was not enough to have "the cup" of God's wrath, judgment, and death to be averted. Yes, Jesus glorified God in suffering and death, but He was not delivered from the cross. Prayer may not make adversity just go away.

Be sure not to let conflict and suffering determine your agenda. There are Christians who don't attend church when they are sick, "feeling poorly," or find themselves exhausted from work. It was quite the opposite in the early church.

First-century believers went to church *because* they were sick. It was where people prayed and preachers preached that healing occurred. There are no Bible accounts about people getting healed because they stayed away from church. Many were healed because they were with God's people, in the middle of God's activity.

Even if God chooses to remove the adversity, it may not occur right away. If there were immediate solutions, people wouldn't pray or draw near to God. Some conflicts cannot be instantly resolved.

> We ourselves who have the Spirit as the firstfruits — we also groan within ourselves,

eagerly waiting for adoption, the redemption of our bodies. (Romans 8:23 HCSB)

Atonement for sin was completed on the cross, but immediate relief from the world won't be experienced fully until believers are at home in heaven. The same is true for the conflicts and adversities that assail you. Pray that God would remove them, but be prepared to draw even closer to God if they are not.

In Times of Adversity Go to the Word of God

> All Scripture is inspired by God and is useful to teach us what is true and to make us realize what is wrong in our lives. It corrects us when we are wrong and teaches us to do what is right. God uses it to prepare and equip his people to do every good work. (2 Timothy 3:16–17 NLT)

The Bible is God's primary method of speaking to you. It's impossible to respond successfully to adversity and disregard the word. You might start by reaffirming the promises of God. Know what they are, and learn to apply them to your own life. Know what the Bible says about the ways and promises of God *before* the crisis. Otherwise you may find yourself reacting in urgent-mode rather than in faith-mode.

You may recall Scriptural events, specific verses, and spiritual principles that apply to your situation. God never reacts out of surprise to our circumstances, and He provided the scripture to teach us His ways.

Adversity is an opportunity to grow in Christ if you apply the Word to your circumstances. God's Word is replete with principles and promises that are able to change your whole perspective and give you the spiritual tools to respond.

5

You Should Employ the Adversity in Ministry to Others

The Christians in Macedonia were tested severely by trials and afflictions, poverty and persecution. But somehow they found the joy they had in Jesus to be enough. Not only that, it spilled over into ministry to others. In their affliction they begged Paul to let them reach out and help others.

> We want you to know, brothers, about the grace of God granted to the churches of Macedonia: During a severe testing by affliction, their abundance of joy and their deep poverty overflowed into the wealth of their generosity. I testify that, on their own, according to their ability and beyond their ability, they begged us insistently for the privilege of sharing in the ministry to the saints, and not just as we had hoped. Instead, they gave themselves especially to the Lord, then to us by God's will. (2 Corinthians 8:1–5 HCSB)

Darril Deaton

The Christians at Philippi often helped Paul on his journeys and through his difficulties. He wrote and told them:

> Not one church shared with me in the matter of giving and receiving, except you only; for even when I was in Thessalonica, you sent me aid again and again when I was in need. (Philippians 4:15–16 NIV)

As you can see from this letter, Paul's emphasis was on the act of giving. It's the nature of the *act*, not the nature of the *gift*, that is important.

Adversity may be the very platform of ministry for you. While you look for a sterile, domesticated, civilized place of ministry, it may be in the trenches of adversity, humility, and pain that God provides your greatest chance to benefit others. When you bless others, it opens the door for God to bless you. You should comfort others, not in spite of your adversary but because of it!

> [God] comforts us in all our affliction, so that we may be able to comfort those who are in any kind of affliction, through the comfort we ourselves receive from God. (2 Corinthians 1:3–4 HCSB)

There's one important thing you should know about praying for others. God wants everyone to trust in Jesus Christ and have eternal life. Adversity will often pressure an unbeliever to call upon God and give Him serious consideration. It may be that when you pray for an unbelieving relative or friend, adversity turns out to be the answer to your prayer. If adversity is what it would take for a person to be drawn to God, He may very well allow him or her to face all kinds of problems. Seeking to bless another person will sometimes open the door for adversity and trials in his or her life. But if that person embraces the gospel as a result, it will have been worth it.

6

Whatever You Do, Whatever Happens, Praise the Lord!

Shout for joy in the LORD, O you righteous! Praise befits the upright. (Psalm 33:1 ESV)

I t is always fitting to praise the Lord! There is never a circumstance so difficult or a valley so deep that God should not be praised. It makes little difference what the source of your adversity is. The issue is how you respond to it, and praise is always an appropriate response.

God is just as worthy of praise today as He was yesterday. Even though your circumstances may have changed, the Creator has not changed. Glory will always reside in the Father no matter what your circumstances.

Thank God for *not* letting you get by with living your life apart from Him. God is personally interested in you. That is why adversity is tailor-made to fit your individual spiritual needs.

Praise God for conforming you to the image of His Son, Jesus Christ. Thank Him for the pressure of adversity that makes it happen.

Part 4

Where Do Good Things Come From?

We have seen that there are three sources of adversity: sin, Satan, and God. But life isn't always filled with conflicts and trouble. There are times when we experience some very good things.

Sometimes we are just relieved when a conflict is resolved. Other times we may receive an unexpected blessing or benefit right out of the blue. Blessings, like adversities, have a source and a divine outcome. So, where do these good things come from? Why should God give you anything at all? How should you respond to the good things God gives you?

1

God Is the One and Only Source of Good Things

> Every good gift and every perfect gift is from above, coming down from the Father of lights with whom there is no variation or shadow due to change. (James 1:17 ESV)

Your life, like creation, is not an accident. You are not the product of circumstances or an accident of nature. Remember, even when God allows adversity and conflict, evil and pain, it is to accomplish something holy in your life. The same is true for the good things that happen to you, too.

Satan would be glad to take credit for the good things. He really doesn't always want to be known for doing evil. He would make you filthy rich if he thought you'd take your eyes off of Jesus. So-called blessings are not always an indicator that God favors you.

A closer look at James 1:17 will prove helpful. In the original language the word *good* literally means something useful or something of value. It doesn't have to be new to be of value. As you know, antiques often have great value.

The word for *gift* is more about the act of giving and the intention of the giver. A child's artwork may not make it into the Louvre in Paris, but to the parent for whom it is made, it is a masterpiece.

> Yet it was good of you to share in my troubles. Moreover, as you Philippians know, in the early days of your acquaintance with the gospel, when I set out from Macedonia, not one church shared with me in the matter of giving and receiving, except you only; for even when I was in Thessalonica, you sent me aid again and again when I was in need. (Philippians 4:14–15 NIV)

Paul emphasized the love behind the act of giving. It's the nature of the act, not the nature of the gift that matters.

The word for *perfect* is about doing something the right way. It meets the real needs of the recipient, not just his or her desires. It's about the physical, emotional, mental, or spiritual needs of a person.

Usually men talk of perfection in terms of meeting or exceeding a standard of some kind, like an athletic event in which an athlete strives to meet or break a record. But for God, perfection means that He sets the standard. He *is* the standard.

> For all have sinned and fall short of the glory of God … (Romans 3:23 ESV)

God is the standard we've all fallen short of. His gifts far exceed your abilities. And the fact that good things are *from above* indicates that God's gifts are not of earthly origin. Jesus said that to see the kingdom of God you must be born *from above*. Your salvation depends on God's gift of eternal life that comes not from earth, but from Him.

Every good thing literally means every good thing— not some good things or even most good things. There isn't one good thing that you or Satan can give that is perfect and eternal. You and the devil are sources of adversity, conflict, turmoil, and pain, but never a source of lasting, useful, eternal things.

> But if you have bitter jealousy and selfish ambition in your hearts, do not boast and be false to the truth. This is not the wisdom that comes down from above, but is earthly, unspiritual, demonic. For where jealousy and selfish ambition exist, there will be disorder and every vile practice. (James 3:14–16 ESV)

God created a wonderful, beautiful world. It was an act of genius, grace, and order. Sin, your sin, results in chaos, pain, and death. Your conflicts, trials, heartaches, and tears find their source in humanity. You have to depend upon God for all the good things.

> So one rendering of James 1:17 could be:
>
> Every beneficial act of giving that is done, in the way that it ought to be done, to meet the

real needs that people have, is from the One and only absolute standard in the universe. (James 1:17 DVR)

Jesus died on the cross to meet you at your point of need. He is God's solution to the separation that exists between you and the God who loves you. Again the genius, grace, and wonder of God are demonstrated.

Even after your sin disrupts God's divine glory, He proves His benevolence, His goodness, and His love by providing the best gift of all: salvation out the chaos and darkness of Jesus's death.

2

Why Does God Give You Anything At All?

I t isn't because He owes it to you! It's not because you deserve it! And it isn't because He is a benevolent Santa-God who saves everyone. God is the Source of good things because He loves you!

> For *God loved* the world in this way: *He gave* His One and Only Son, so that everyone who believes in Him will not perish but have eternal life. (John 3:16 HCSB)

Agape love is a giving love. It's what you need, not just what you want. Your need was for a Savior, so you got one! You can talk about answered prayers, wonders of nature, multiple blessings, and God's mighty deeds, but you can never understand the significance of all these things without viewing God through the perspective of the cross. Yes, God is the one and only source of good things in your life because He loves you.

3

How Should You Respond to the Good Things God Gives You?

Rejoice in the Lord always. I will say it again: Rejoice! ... Do not be anxious about anything, but in everything, by prayer and petition, with thanksgiving, present your requests to God. And the peace of God, which transcends all understanding, will guard your hearts and your minds in Christ Jesus. Finally, brothers, whatever is true, whatever is noble, whatever is right, whatever is pure, whatever is lovely, whatever is admirable—if anything is excellent or praiseworthy—think about such things. Whatever you have learned or received or heard from me, or seen in me—put it into practice. And the God of peace will be with you. (Philippians 4:4–9 NIV)

*R*espond through prayer. Talk to the God who loves you more than anything. Be thankful. Express heartfelt gratefulness to God, not just for the good things, but even for the conflicts that shape your character to be more like Jesus.

Direct your thoughts to excellent and praiseworthy things. Try not to let worldly distractions keep you from focusing your thoughts on good things, on good people, and on good memories.

Whatever God gives you, give it back. Yes, give it back to God through others. God will supply you with resources if He knows you will share it and not hoard it.

> God is able to make all grace abound to you, so that in all things at all times, having all that you need, you will abound in every good work ... You will be made rich in every way *so that you can be generous* on every occasion, and through us you generosity will result in thanksgiving to God. (2 Corinthians 9:8, 11 NIV)

Our resources often dry up because the supply is cut off. When you hoard God's blessings and keep them all to yourself, God may stop the flow of resources altogether. He supplies everything you need so you can be generous. It's a cycle of blessing from God, to you, to others. If it stops with you ... well, it stops.

God gives you grace, love, healing, wisdom, friends, resources, and more because He loves you. Even the adversities of life are a gift from God. The spiritual believer is able to understand why things happen the way they do and respond correctly.

As you grow in Christ, and strengthen your intimate relationship to Him, you will respond correctly to adversity. You should be so secure in the love of God that nothing, absolutely nothing, will be able to steal you away from your walk with Him.

Final Thoughts

Jesus said, "You will have suffering in this world. Be courageous! I have conquered the world" (John 16:33 HCSB).

Nowhere does God promise you a trouble-free life. True Christ-followers, of all people, should not be surprised that troubles and affliction are a part of life. Over and over again in the Bible you are not threatened with the possibility of adversity—it is promised to you.

There's no guarantee that the sick will be healed or all your financial needs will be met, that all your prayers will be answered in the affirmative, or that life will be easier because you're a Christian. This is not the case, regardless of what charlatans and some so-called evangelists say. To the contrary, Jesus guaranteed that believers would have suffering in the world. Period. It's a necessary part of your experience here. And it's a part of your most fruitful ministry too.

In addition to that, Jesus said you were to be courageous in the face of conflict, suffering, and distress. Of course having actually seen heaven, Jesus had a perspective that you don't naturally have. Heaven is not your default frame of reference. The Bible, however, tells you much about heaven, your future, and even how the present darkness ends in light, joy, and relief. Jesus calls you to be courageous until then. He can tell you that because He has overcome the world ... including all its trials and tribulations.

Nothing happens that isn't first sifted through the perfect will of God. He is never caught off guard. God never says, "Oops, I sure didn't see that coming!" He is never caught by surprise.

Try to determine why things happen the way they do. Pray and seek God's wisdom. It's okay to bring your doubts and fears to Him. Just be open to the lessons He wants to teach you or the ministry He wants to lead you into.

Commit your way to Him, and always give Him praise. He is still as worthy of praise in your adversity as He was before it occurred and after it passes. And yes, it will pass, if not in this life then in your life to come in heaven.

Everything happens for a reason. If you respond the right way—God's way—then you won't waste the experience or get another go-round with unnecessary adversity until you "get it." God will fully utilize the conflicts you suffer and the adversity you endure for His purposes and your good.

No matter how dark and painful your trials may be— no matter what the reason may be for the bad things that happen—another look at the cross should convince you that God always has your best interest in mind and that He loves you.

❧ ❧